I FOUGHT THE LAW
and
I WON

Charles F. Johnson

I Fought the Law and I Won
Copyright © 2019 by Charles F. Johnson

Library of Congress Control Number: 2019915364
    ISBN-13: Paperback: 978-1-950073-85-6
    ePub: 978-1-950073-86-3

All rights reserved. No part of this publication may be reproduced, distributed, or transmitted in any form or by any means, including photocopying, recording, or other electronic or mechanical methods, without the prior written permission of the publisher or author, except in the case of brief quotations embodied in critical reviews and certain other noncommercial uses permitted by copyright law.

Although every precaution has been taken to verify the accuracy of the information contained herein, the author and publisher assume no responsibility for any errors or omissions. No liability is assumed for damages that may result from the use of information contained within.

Printed in the United States of America

GoToPublish LLC
1-888-337-1724
www.gotopublish.com
info@gotopublish.com

DEDICATION

I would like to dedicate this book to my late mother. Dorotha M. Johnson. It was she that gave me the courage, strength, love and most of all support. With this powerful drive behind me I knew that with the grace of God I could tackle this monumental feat and come out a winner. She died in 1997 before she could witness my triumph, but I know that when she left this world she left me the wisdom and faith to continue to victory.

I know she is looking down and has told me many times how proud she is of her son.

As the new Millennium has arrived old employment practices still exist. There are over 146 million employed people in the United States and every 3 seconds one of them is discriminated against. Employees go to work to do their assigned jobs and only want to be treated as equals and human beings. On the other hand "Employers" or Supervisors or Managers, whatever title they carry, have other ideas in mind.

I Fought the Law and I Won

I was hired by the United States Department of Agriculture as a disabled Veteran in the fall 1991 as a Procurement Clerk. GS-4. Being a Disable Veteran I received what the government calls, "10 Point Veteran's Preference". This allows newly hired Veterans extra 10 points on their government rating scale. The government gives numerical grades or numbers to applicants for their KSA's. This stands for Knowledge, Skills, and Abilities. It is this total score which determines if you are qualified for the position that you are applying for. Being a Disabled Veteran gives you the additional advantage of 10 additional points added onto your final score.

This additional 10 points that I received was to be the festering wound that my CO-workers later used to try to destroy my career and eventually my life.

In March of 1992 I was promoted to a Purchasing Agent, a GS-5. I was the only male in an all-female office of eight. I shared an office with two female Purchasing Agents, of which we all had our on cubicle.

After a long week at work the office would get together at a local pub to unwind. My immediate supervisor. Jane would not attend as she had young children that she needed to attend to at home. Our first line supervisor. Grace as GS-11 would attend. I basically got along with everyone in my department. My immediate supervisor, Jane and I got along great. The first line supervisor, Grace and I did have some different views on certain subjects. Grace was our new Administration Officer just reassigned and promoted to our office. As all newly appointed officers, they try to start their new position with getting to know a little bit about their employees.

On several occasions when we got together after work, the rest of the office would leave Grace and me alone. The first couple of times she made unusual remarks in a sexual nature; I just shrugged it off as a joke. These remarks got more personal and more sexual each week we met at the pub. She would go into explicit detail about her private life and the troubles she was having with her family. Of course being the tentative person that I am, I listened with great interest. These private drinking sessions got more personal and more detailed as time went on.

Around the first of February 1992 Grace lowered the boom. After all these sexual advancements failed she grew more irritated and angry towards me. Then she made her move. She informed me thatif I didn't commit myself to her she could make it very hard on me at work. She went into great detail as to what she could do to make my working for the USDA a living hell.

Being completely floored and caught off guard I answered with the first thing that came to my mind.

"Your fat, Your Ugly, and I would rather sleep with a dog then sleep with you". At this point she crudely gathered her things and stormed out of the pub. I didn't know what to think or do so I left the pub and went home called a very close friend of mine to tell her what had just happened. My friend being as close as we are was totally shocked at what I had just told her. I ask her, "What she thought I should do"? She said, "That I should just ignore what had just happened and go to work on the Monday and act like nothing happened". I spent the entire weekend racking my brain as to what just happened, and what I was going to do about it. So I just put this incident in the back of my mind and forgot about it.

I returned to work the following Monday to find a cold, callous Grace snarling at my every move. She had turned from an Administrative Officer to an employer from Hell. I was shell-shocked to see the difference in the two people that I knew. I had made up my mind that I was not going to let this incident interfere with my work performance. I carried on like I had always done and did my job to the best of my ability.

After a couple of weeks the other people in my office began to act peculiar towards me. I couldn't figure out why. They were not their

I Fought the Law and I Won

friendly out-going selves that I had come to know. It was if someone had poisoned their minds against me. They didn't say good morning anymore, they didn't invite me to join their lunch groups, and they had just flatly written me of as a bad debt.

At the end of April 1992 I approached my supervisor, Jane reminding her that my six-month probationary period was up and that I wanted my review so that I could get my grade GS-6. Sheasked me if I could wait till the end of the government's fiscal year buying was over and then she would give me my review. This being the busiest time of the year for us. I agreed.

Around June first I approached her and requested again my review. She replied that she had to talk to Grace, her supervisor first. So I figured that I would give her time to do so.

On or about July 15, 1992 I went over Jane's head and went straight to Grace's office. I came to the point and ask why my appraisal was not forthcoming? She reared back in her seat like a wounded animal and bellowed. "If you qualify for the next grade then you'll get it". I replied, "I do qualify for the next grade, so when do I get it"?

She shuffled some papers around on her desk, slid her chair back and forth on the floor, knowing all along that she was trying to put me off and not give me an answer, I figured I was getting nowhere. I thanked her politely turned around and left her office.

Knowing that I was not going to get any satisfaction from her I decided to go over her head. The next day I called the main personnel office in charge of our division and wanted know what my next move was pertaining to this matter. After talking to a Personnel Specialist I was informed that I was eligible for the performance appraisal and thus qualified for the next grade level. I ask this person, "What was the next step in the chain of command"? They told me to speak to my immediate supervisor. They suggested that I present to her a copy of the Personnel Manual pertaining to this matter. So I looked up in the USDA Regulations and found the section pertaining to this matter.

The next day I went back to my supervisor Jane and reiterated what the Personnel Department had informed me, plus I gave her a copy of the USDA regulations dealing with this matter. She read the regulation, looked at me with this pale dull expression on her face and said nothing. I then ask her, "What are you going to do about this"? Before I could get the words out of my mouth, she reached in her desk and pulled out this piece of paper and handed it to me and said please sign this. Being elated thinking that this was my performance appraisal, I glanced down and said, "What is this"? "This isn't a performance appraisal, this is a performance plan". She replied, "Yes and after 90 days we will give you your performance appraisal". She said that Grace told her to give this to me. I angrily replied. "I have been a purchasing agent for over 9 months now, and I am just now getting a performance plan"?

I reminded her that I should have been given this plan 9 months ago when I started as an agent. She reluctantly agreed but shyly said, "That's what Grace told me to do". At this point I informed her that I was going to the head of Personnel and file a formal complaint against Grace, not her. I told her, there were no hard feelings against her but I had to go over her head.

Before I called Agriculture Personnel. I called my counselor at the Veterans Administration and ask his opinion on what I should do. He immediately replied, "Mr. Johnson you have been screwed and don't let them do this to you".

The Veterans Administration has employment counselors that are there just for incidents like this. He explained exactly what they were trying to do to me and at the same time they instructed me as to what my next actions should be.

The next day I called the Head of Personnel and he was not in, so I was directed to his subordinate Sarah, who also was not in and I finally ended up with a man named Charlie. I ran my story down to Charlie and he agreed that I was denied due process on my complaint. He told me not to do anything, that he would call my first line supervisor Grace and get this problem resolved.

I Fought the Law and I Won

The first of August I called back to Personnel and spoke to Charlie and ask him, "What was being done about my problem"? He said, "I talked to Grace and told her she was wrong and that you deserved your performance appraisal now". Then after a long pause he said, "But after you receive it you might not want to sign it". I ask, "What does that mean"? He said, "Someone will be talking to you soon".

On or about August 4, 1992, Sarah called me from Labor Relations and said she wanted to meet with me. On August 5, 1992 I went to Labor Relations office and met with Sarah. SURPRISE! SURPRISE! SURPRISE!

Sarah informed me that she had received a complaint against me. She proceeded to read off a list of erroneous complaints field against me by none other than Grace. The Charges being: (1) Mr. Johnson was overheard by his office CO-Worker, Ms. Jones telling a vendor from Advanced Computers, during the competitive phase of a procurement, that if he (Mr. James) "ate" his shipping charges that he would be the lowest bidder and thus receive the contract.

(2) Mr. Johnson has been observed showing vendor copies of the competitive documents from all responding vendors, prior to the award of the competitive contract. (3) Mr. Johnson has been overheard repeatedly suggesting to vendors that their chances of being awarded contracts would be much better if they were to take him out for drinks. It was at this point I became furious and knew that all these allegations were filed by none other than Grace. Of course I couldn't believe my ears, all lies, all vicious rumors that Grace had conjured up along with the rest of my office co-workers. After hearing all these lies I was so mad and I let Sara Know it too.

I told her that Grace had made up all these lies. Because, she couldn't stand being told by the Personnel Department that she was wrong and that she had to give me my performance appraisal.

At this point I wanted to tell her about the sexual advancements but I knew it was Grace's word against mine and with these calculated charges she would never believe me.

Sarah said she would type up this list of complaints and call me back over to make any changes and to discuss what to do next.

Well I remember when I refused Grace's sexual advancements she said, "She would make it hard on me and here it is". I never in my wildest imagination could believe she would make up these allegations and worst of all, get my CO-workers to go along with her.

It was at this very point that I finally realized that I had a big problem on my hands and that I was going to have to fight and fight hard to keep my job.

To Whom It May Concern: give an example of her petty accusations, on or about August 10, 1992 I went to lunch with a co-worker. We signed out for lunch at 12:15PM and signed back in at 12:45PM. At 4:45PM the girl that I went to lunch with came into my office and told me that Grace told her that we had left at 12:00PM instead of 12:15PM and she wanted us to change our time sheets to reflect the ten minute difference, of which we did.

Of course now every other worker in our office could take, as much time as they wanted for lunch, and never had to alter their time sheets.

On or about August 19, 1992 Sarah called from Labor Relations and said, "She had the list of complaints ready for me to go over. I made an appointment to see her on Friday.

On Friday I went to Sarah's office at 7:30AM. I read over the list of complaints and made several corrections in one of the statements, and added a paragraph at the end of the letter. I wrote that all these complaints were false lies, hearsay evidence conjured up by Grace in order to try to get me fired, because she had a personal dislike for me.

I hesitantly signed the letter, plus handed her a 20 page chronological account of every person's whereabouts in Grace's office for the past six months, as my evidence. I then left Sarah's office with a totally new outlook on the Federal Governments Management Program. To think that an Administrator Officer would go through so much detailed

I Fought the Law and I Won

hearsay to get back at someone that refused her sexual advances, was simply a crime in itself.

To try and bolster my excellent work record and add some positive evidence to this injustice being done to me, I wanted to show that I did my job so efficiently that I had received two accommodations from two upper management personnel for outstanding performance in my duties as purchasing agent for the U.S, Government. Withthese two official documents in hand I personally delivered them to Ms. Grace's office and demanded she place these documents in my personnel file. With disgust in her eyes, a snarl on her face, she again reared back in her chair and said, "I'll see that these get placed in your personnel file". I replied, "I know you will because I plan to check in a week to make sure you did".

On or about August 21, 1993 I received a letter from the personnel office congratulating another agent and myself for being chosen to go to St. Louis, Mo., for the advanced purchasing agents training. I was really excited about this trip.

The other agent came to my office about a week later and asks me if I had received my approval for the travel advancements and had I received my voucher number for the airline tickets? I said, "No" I had not received them yet". I then told her that I would look into it further and get back to her.

On September 2, 1992 I was sitting in my office of which I shared with two other agents, working late when Grace entered my office and placed an inner office memo envelope into the outgoing mailbox. As she left my office she looked back over her shoulder and snarled at me like a scalded cat. "BINGO" a light lit up, bells rang in my ears and a mysterious voice in my head said, "get that envelope and open it and read it". So I did! Inside the envelope was an official memo, on Government stationary, singed by Grace to her Boss, subject being Allegations of Impropriety in Charles F. Johnson's position as Purchasing Agent.

This two- page Memo began with all the allegations that she had formally alleged against me with Labor Relations department. I didn't have that much time to read the whole two page memo, but after reading almost the entire first page, when I got to the bottom of the page I read the most chilling, disturbing, degrading and discriminating sentence of my life. After all these false allegations against me she had the nerve to write in this memo to her boss on Official Government Letterhead, "We have a "Flaming Queer", working in our Service Center". Well I almost fell out of my chair. After regaining my composure and catching my breath I realized that this was my big chance to expose Grace for what she really was. After all her sexual advances and the lies she tried to use to get me fired, this was my chance to get justice. I looked around the office to see who was there.

I did not see any of the other workers so I quietly and softly took the Memo across the hall and made a copy of it. I was a nervous wreck, as I knew that Grace was still in the building somewhere. I then placed the original memo back in the envelope and back in the outgoing mailbox.

With this damaging Memo where she was trying to get me fired, she had just called me a "Flaming Queer"

I knew right away that this would be the most damaging evidence that I could possibly have to prove that she had total disregard for my Civil Rights. I immediately called an attorney friend of mine, Mr. Link and briefly explained to him what had been happening to me in the past year. I also told him that I had a copy of this Memo in my hands, where an Administrative Officer of the Federal Government had just called me a "Flaming Queer" He immediately wanted to see the memo and me and to discuss what was later to become one of the biggest Sexual Harassment cases in Government history.

After a long and grueling discussion with my Attorney we both agreed, at this point it was time to file the necessary paper work to initiate a Federal EEO grievance against the United States Government. We charged them with five separate counts of, Age Discrimination, Sexual Harassment, Sexual Discrimination, violation of the VRA (Veterans Re-Adjustment Act), and violation of the Americans with Disabilities Act.

I Fought the Law and I Won

Approximately two weeks after the initial filing of these Grievances, The head Administrator of our Service Center called a meeting. This meeting was short and sweet. He informed us that Grace, our beloved supervisor, was being transferred to another division with the U.S. Government, effective immediately. She left the very next day!

Around January 20, 1993 a Gentleman named Tom, was appointed as acting Administrative Officer temporarily filing Grace's position until a permanent replacement could be found.

While the wheels of the legal system were steadily working on my grievances, life and job went on at the Department of Agriculture. The false charges that Grace originally filed against me were still being processed through the Labor Relations Department, as a disciplinary action.

A week after Tom took office he called me into his office to tell me that we had an appointment with Pete, his Supervisor as 9:30AM the next day. The next day at 9:30AM Tom and I went to Pete's office and sat at this round table where Pete proceeded to explain to me what was going to take place in the near future.

He handed me this stack of papers from the Labor Relations Department and informed me that these were the charges that Grace had filed against me. He read from these papers that said. "The Labor Relations Department has recommended a 14 day suspension. (without pay) for these allegations" alleged against you. Of course he stated that this was just a recommendation and I had 15 days to reply to the accusations.

At this point Pete informed me that because of the allegations and the nature of my position, he found it necessary to detail me out of my purchasing agent's position, to the warehouse. He also informed me that he had canceled the training classes that I was to take in St. Louis.

Amazing, at this point Pete informed Tom and I that he had also accepted another position in New York and was leaving immediately. Coincidence, Pete just happened to be Grace's Supervisor, of whom the infamous memo was sent to.

After hearing this earth shattering news I tried to regain my composure and try not to lose my temper. I suddenly felt awful hot and my heart was racing out of my chest. I stood up, with wobbling knees and informed both Pete and Tom that I was not feeling well and that I was going downstairs to my office and fill out a leave slip and go to the VA Hospital Emergency room.

I left work immediately and went directly to the Veterans Hospital's emergency room where I sat uncomfortably waiting to see a doctor. I was finally ushered into an exam room where I wasseen by my Cardiologist Dr. Groom, I explained to him what had happened at work. He gave me an EKG and checked my heart rate and blood pressure. He found them both to be extremely high. He said, "You must have encountered something really bad to causeyour vital signs to go this extremely high".

He gave me a shot to help slow down my heart rate. He then gave me two types of medication to take, then he ordered me to go straight home and go to bed. He also gave me strict instructions not to return to work for several days. I took a total of four days off to recuperate.

On February 2, 1993 I reported to the warehouse as ordered at 7:30AM. The supervisor of the warehouse, Dave, greeted me. I explained to Dave that I was a 40% disabled Veteran with Severe Carpal Tunnel Syndrome, and that I could not lift anything over 2 pounds. He immediately took offense and replied, "This is a warehouse, blue collar work". We load and unload large trucks of supplies. We lift articles over 75 pounds, and fill large orders for the entire Department of Agriculture. He remarked, "Why would they send someone with a disability here to work in the warehouse?"

For the first couple of days I was told only to fill small orders of supplies for the administrative offices. This I could do without any discomfort. I arrived at work every day on time and left work every day on time, as I was directed. My being detailed there really placed a psychological barrier between the warehouse employees and myself. I knew that they resented me because I was given preferential treatment.

I Fought the Law and I Won

During the next two months at the warehouse my legal procedures were starting to work. After my lawyer and doctors contracted the appropriate officials at the Headquarters of the Department of Agriculture and informed them of the ramifications that would follow if I were not removed from the warehouse. Then I was removed from the warehouse.

On April 1, 1993 I was detailed to the Health and Safety Office where I was to become the, temporary Hazardous Waste Technician. This was a clerical position with a private office, where there were no other employees around me. I was pleased and happy with thisnew assignment and glad to be back in the administrative field.

On May 18, 1993 I filed a formal Workers Compensation Claim for aggravation of my Carpal Tunnel Syndrome which stemmed from the detail to the Warehouse. This claim was for the purpose of future hospitalization and or additional medical treatment that I might need.

On June 30, 1993 my Workers Compensation claim was approved for any and all future medical claims of my disability with Severe Carpal Tunnel Syndrome.

After almost a year and a half had past, on July 14, 1993 I finally received my Performance Appraisal reflecting my previous position as a Purchasing Agent. Remembering, this Performance Appraisal being the original issue for my complaint against my former first line Supervisor, Grace.

Coincidentally my new detailed position in the Safety and Health office now just happens to be down the hall from where my old position as a Purchasing Agent was. Jane, my original supervisor brought the appraisal to me in my new office for me to sign. She was really glad to see me and told me that there were no hard feelings towards her, because it was Grace not her that violated my Civil Rights.

As I read the appraisal, much to my surprise, I saw that she had given me an outstanding rating on my overall performance as a Purchasing Agent.

With this in mind, I reminded that I still have that 14-day suspension foe improprieties in my job, for which she has just given me an outstanding evaluation. I made the comment, "that makes no sense, does it"? With both of us sort of smirking silently, I was more than happy to finally sign this appraisal. I also said, "Now you see if Grace had only admitted that she was wrong, and didn't make matters worse by referring to me in a sexual manner, this whole mess would have never happened"?

I have always wanted to only do my job the best of my ability and never receive anything that I did not deserve.

To cover the Agencies backside and try to comply with the EEO Laws, a very strong Memo was circulated to all employees at the agency level. The memo from Dr. Finny, Acting Administrator stated, "Derogatory remarks of a sexual or racial nature will not be tolerated by any employee of the Department of Agriculture. Anyone caught making such remarks will be disciplined and or removed from the Agency".

I spent the next year at the Safety Office always maintaining an outstanding performance. I grew and learned many new things while in this position. It was just another brick in the wall for me. I have always enjoyed broadening my horizons in whatever jobs I maintained.

My supervisor at the safety office was very pleased with my performance, so much that she recommended to her supervisor that I be given this position permanently.

During this very eventful year my five EEO cases were making their way through the Federal network of regulations. I attended three Dispute and Resolution hearings at the Department of Agriculture's downtown Washington, DC office.

I also attended three or four personnel administrative hearings, which were held in the different locations throughout the agency. During and after all these hearings it was very obvious that the Government knew that they had a very serious problem on their hands.

I Fought the Law and I Won

At the time of these hearings the Government flew in Grace, from down south somewhere, and Pete from somewhere in New York to testify under oath. Both of them lied like rugs. Grace trying to put the blame on Pete and Pete denying he ever talked to Grace. All evidence pointing to both of them as being the guilty parties.

I don't know why all this administrative BULL even took place. It was obvious the government had to take responsibility for their actions, but never once punished any of these individuals involved with lying and cover-ups.

On June 1, 1993 the alleged charges filed against me by Grace finally made their way through the Government's red tape and I was found guilty of inappropriate conduct as a Purchasing Agent. No matter what defense I used, either the fact that I received an Outstanding Appraisal for this period, or the fact that I had 5EEO grievances filed against them, I was still suspended for 14 days without pay.

The Government knew they were beaten at their own game. They knew that they had broken every law that were sworn to uphold and still they railroad me with this 14-day suspension. Well I took it like a man!

Returning to work on June 15, 1993, as if I had just been on a vacation, I was overwhelmed by the greeting that I received from my co-workers in the Safety Office. It seemed they actually missed me and the work piled up on my desk was proof. So like the storm trooper I am, I immediately got back to work as usual.

I really enjoyed this position at the Safety Office, because it allowed me many hours outside where I could get away from it all. I was fortunate to be able to get out and enjoy the beautiful scenery of the 7,000 acres of farmland at the Beltsville facility.

The physical location of my office in the Safety department was right down the hall from my previous job as the Purchasing Agent. On my occasions I found it necessary to walk down the hall towards my old office and of course I would come face to face with those other women that plotted against me to have me fired.

I held my head up high and looked them all right in the eye as we passed, and never would they look at me. They were so filled with guilt that they looked at the floor and sometimes they would even dart in adjoining offices to avoid me altogether. I always knew in my heart that I had done nothing to warrant the treatment that I received from those co-workers, but my life as it was went on.

This position that I held in the Safety Office was supposed to be only a detail, which is a temporary position that lasts one year at most. On or about December of 1993 my Supervisor Carolynn came to me and said that come April my detail would be up and that she wanted me to apply for the position permanently. I was so thrilled that she had actually asked me to stay on that I almost cried. So I told her that I would officially apply for the position.

I filled out the necessary paper work and submitted it to Personnel, Sometime in January of 1994 I received a call from the Personnel office, pertaining to my application for this position. They indicated that I did not have the education requirements to qualify for this position but since I had performed this position for at least one year at a satisfactory rate that this requirement could be waived, if management approved. Now that was the magic phrase! "If management approved"? Now having been introduced to the Federal Governments own management of the Federal Law, which they are supposed to uphold, I was not prepared for what I was about to receive, If I thought the infamous memo from Grace was a violation of my Civil rights, then this next was the gospel,"Good Book".

Early in February 1994 management sent me yet another infamous "Memo". On Government Stationary and officially signed by someone in Management saying, "Mr. Johnson, we have reviewed your application for the Position of Waste Management Technician and we find that your education does not meet the qualifications forthis position. However, we will waive this requirement, and give you a promotion with grade increase, if you agree to withdraw all five of your EEO Grievances against the United States Government!" Well, all I could think is I can't believe that they are actually saying this to me. My next thought was, "Hello", does anyone out there knowthe term BLACKMAIL?

I Fought the Law and I Won

Well of course I called my attorney and he had the same reaction that I did and he told me to fax him immediately a copy of this Memo. At this time my attorney filed EEO Grievance number six (6), for just as I had stated, for "BLACKMAIL" "A FELONY FEDERAL OFFENSE"

After this latest grievance was filed with the Department of Agriculture in Washington D.C., Management immediately sent me another Memo informing me that their previous offer was being withdrawn. I guess somebody finally woke up!

Now of course by now we have 6 EEO grievances, all violations of Federal Statutes and laws filed with the Department of Agriculture and the United States District Attorney's Office.

This is when I really started to feel the pressure. The head supervisor of Safety and Health department started treating me different. He wasn't the friendly out going person that he used to be.

My CO-workers were telling me the gossip going around. My supervisor, Carolynn even said they were putting pressure on her. They all were saying that I had put management in deep trouble. My response was, "Can you believe that Federal Management levels at GS-14 and 15 would purposely break Federal laws that they weresworn to uphold?" I also said, "It was obvious that management has been breaking these laws for a long time and getting away with it". How long did Management think they could commit felonies and violate peoples Civil Rights?

The Civil Rights Act of 1964 was enacted to protect the civil rights of all Americans in the work place. This law was enacted so that just what had happened to me, would be illegal and make management accountable for their actions. I just happened to be the person that was discriminated against and I was mad. I am fighting back and management doesn't like it.

By this time we had several more EEO administrative hearings held at the Dispute Resolution Board located in Washington, DC to try and settle these grievances. At the last DRB hearing scheduled, was when the Government made a last ditch effort to squash these proceedings by making an offer of settlement. Of course knowing the magnitude of these charges and the compensatory damages that I could gain, there was no way we would accept their offer. So, their offer was rejected and we advised them that all their avenues of appeal were exhausted and we would see them in Federal Court.

A few days after the settlement rejection, I received two things from management to show good faith.

(1) A letter from the Area Director where he said, "I am sorry that you feel you were sexually harassed by someone at the USDA".

"We at the Management level do not tolerate such actions". Noticing nowhere in the Memo, did he admit that someone in management was found guilty of sexual discrimination, only, that I felt like someone had discriminated against me?

(2) As of April 1, 1994 I was being reassigned as an Accounting Technician with a promotion and grade increase to another service center.

After reading the job description of an Accounting Technician I found out that this position requires 80% of the employee's day doing data entry on the computer. With my disability of Severe Carpal Tunnel Syndrome, there was no way I could sit and type seven (7) hours a day. This would be in direct violation of my hiring status as a Disabled American Veteran, under the Veterans Rehabilitation Act and the Americans with Disabilities Act.

I immediately called my attorney and he fired off a letter to management where he reminded them of my 40% Veterans disability and the fact that this re-assignment position I could not physically perform. Well he might as well have sent that letter to the trash. Management never addressed this issue and on April 1, 1994 I arrived at my new assignment. Remembering at all times the cardinal sin of the Government. They want you to refuse a directorder, they want you to not show up for work, and they want you to give them any excuse at all to terminate you. Well I wasn't going to give them their excuse.

I Fought the Law and I Won

I figured I would let the avenues of Justice take its course and in the meantime I followed orders.

From the first day I arrived at the new Service Center, I felt the tension in the air. My first line supervisor; Iris was very pleasant and right to the point.

She explained to me my duties and I informed her that I was Handicapped and that I could not do data entry for (7) hours a day.

She expressed her sorrow about my disability, but reminded me that this particular position did require at least seven (7) of the eight (8) hours a day doing data entry. She asked me, "Of course you have told management of this condition"? I replied, "I don't know if you know about my legal matter pending in the Federal Courts or not and yes they know about my disability". She replied. "Just between you and me, I have heard something about your EEO cases, but I don't know any details". I then told her that it was best that she not know the details so that she wouldn't get into trouble with my new Administrative Officer, named Mazoo!

As it turned out the Administrative Officer in charge, Mazoo just happened to be best friends with my former and accused boss, Grace. So right from the very beginning I knew my days here at this Service Center were numbered.

What a fluke of luck, my first day at this new and potential deadly job just happened to fall on April 1st. "April fool's Day"!

This particular office also had nine (9) women and one man, myself. As I previously stated my first line supervisor, Iris was very helpful and kind. She worked with me for the first few days to get me acquainted with their system. As she found out I was a very fast learner and didn't have to be told twice to do anything. The problem was I couldn't sit for seven (7) straight hours and type.

One of the women in this office, we'll call her Agnes, was the administrative clerk who sat right outside Mazoo's office. She and

Mazoo were inseparable. In the military we had a name for people like Agnes, "Snitch"! Believe me, she was just that too! "A BIG SNITCH"!

I sat in a cubicle in the next room from Agnes's desk. All phones in the entire building could be accessed from Agnes's phone. Whenever I got a call on my phone, Agnes knew it. It seemed that this girl never left her desk and watched those phones like a hawk. She documented every call coming in and going out. She kept a spiral note pad on her desk that was filled at the end of every day with every note she kept. If for some reason she had to leave her desk, that note pad went with her. Of course the only time she did leave that desk was to spy on someone.

This once old house, which was converted into offices, had many rooms in it and also had a very nice kitchen. All of the employees could keep their lunches in the refrigerator. It also had a coffeepot for everyone to use. This kitchen was right around the corner from my cubicle. Across the hall from that was the bathroom. So everything in this office setting was real close to Agnes. Of course at first I didn't realize that every move I made was being watched and documented. My first line supervisor Iris, even went so far as to tell that every word I spoke was being listened to. She repeated many times to me that these walls have ears. Whenever she came to my cubicle to talk, it was strictly business, because she was afraid of the little snitch too.

We had an in house computer network that allowed us to communicate with each other over the internet. This was one of Mazzo's brilliant ideas, to minimize walking to one another's office or cubicle.

Iris had explained to me, the phones can be eavesdropped on, but to get a message off some ones Internet, you had to go to that person's computer and retrieve the message. So that made it harder for Agnes to snoop.

Well it only took me a couple of days to figure out what was in store for me and it didn't take Agnes long before she showed her ugly head. It seemed that every time I would move and inch in my cubicle, she would pop her head around the corner to see what the noise as. She never hid the fact that she was spying on me.

I Fought the Law and I Won

In the front office where Agnes sat, was a sign in and out board, where we signed in and out every time we arrived or left the office, which included lunch. Of course, we only had a half an hour for lunch which, is either at the office or eating out.

I usually brought my lunch to work, so as not to give Agnes any ammunition to run and tell Mazoo that I took too long for lunch.

In the meantime the legal papers that my Attorney filed with the USDA about my physical inability's to perform this job had finally hit home.

After arriving at work one day I get a call on my phone from Agnes stating that Mazoo wants to see me in her office. So, I go to Mazoo's office and she proceeds to inform me.

"Since you have this disability and your job requires you to perform much more then you are capable of doing, I don't want you to overdo it, so you do what you can and that will be all right". Of course I couldn't believe my ears, she's actually being civilized to me. I said, "Thank you" and left. When leaving Mazoo's office and passing the snitches desk, Agnes gave me the stupidest grin I think I have ever seen. That grin was a warning sign of what was to come next.

Sometime during the next week I had to go out of the office for a few minutes, so I went on my lunchtime. I signed out on the board at let's say 12:00 noon. I returned at 12:30PM (I thought) and signed back in. Of course this is one of the many days when Mazzo would leave the office and never return till the next day. This is when Agnes did her best snooping.

For someone who was supposed to be an Administrative Officer of this office, Mazoo spent more time away from the office then she did at the office. But, do not fear, she had her trusty snitch, Agnes, to watch the fort while she was gone. You can be on old Agnes not to miss a step you made, or a call on the phone, or even when you went to the bathroom.

The next day when Mazoo finally showed up for work, she called me in her office again and said, "Mr. Johnson it has been brought to my attention that you took an extra eight (8) minutes for lunch yesterday". She said, "You signed out at 12:00 noon and signed back in at 12:30PM, when you really returned at 12:38PM" You have to make an adjustment to your time sheet.

Do you want to take these eight (8) minutes as annual leave, or what? I replied, "Whatever you think best, I am flexible". So leaving her office I had to stop by Agnes's desk and fill out a leave slip for those eight (8) minutes. Of course, the snitch was just glowing with glee as I filled out the leave slip. She just couldn't be any happier, knowing that she couldn't wait to run and tell Mazoo that I took the extra eight minutes for lunch.

After all the harassment that I have been taking from the beginning of this nightmare to this down right humiliation that I was receiving form this new supervisor, I was starting to come unglued. I think that at this point they were actually starting to get to me. I did not want to let myself believe that maybe I couldn't take any more of this treatment.

I knew in my heart that if I let them know that they were getting to me that it would be all over for me. I kept saying to myself, hang in there, there is a light at the end of this tunnel. I was constantly throwing up, I couldn't eat, and my nerves were shot. I couldn't sleep at night and when I did get to sleep, I had the worst nightmares you could imaging. For once in my life, I really hated going to work. I thought that I was a much stronger person that this, but I suppose we all have a breaking point.

During the middle of May 1994, under my doctor's orders I started seeing a Psychiatrist to try to help me deal with this situation. My attorney recommended Dr. Elizabeth Lilly. I started seeing her on a regular basis. She had given me medication for Depression and Anxiety.

This mental torture went on, and got worse, as the months passed. There was not a day that went by that Mazoo didn't call me in her office for one complaint after another. I knew the very minute I showed up at work that every move I made was being monitored. Mind you now, Mazoo was never around to witness any of these allegations, but Agnes was. I was accused of: making personal phone calls, talking on the phone too long to customers, making 26 trips a day to the water fountain, going and spending too much time in the bathroom and not signing in and out properly. The worst being: I have been abusing my sick leave, of which was to keep scheduled doctors' appointments. When you work for the U.S. Government you accrue two types of leave. One being sick leave and the other being annual leave.

I was not abusing my sick leave, as I told her on various occasions. Besides, it was none of her business how much sick leave I took, as long as I had the leave accrued, which I did.

The whole month of April was not as bad as the month of May and pat of June. Mazoo and Agnes did not let up on me once. They were trying and almost succeeded in driving me totally insane. Of course Mazoo was prompted by upper management to do everything in her power to get me to quit. But No I am not a quitter, but a fighter. I will admit though I did make extra doctor appointments, just so I wouldn't have to face those two horrible individuals. In all my 35 years of being employed I had never faced anything like this treatment that I was experiencing. I knew now more than I did before that I couldn't take any more of this torture.

On June 14, 1994 before I could even get into the door. Agnes came running up to me like some little childish schoolgirl and said. "Mazoo wants to see you in her office right now! I didn't even have time to put my things down on my desk. Of course Agnes followed me all the way to Mazoo's office like some sick puppy. I entered Mazoo's office and I shut the door, right in Agnes's face. I walked over to Mazoo's desk and stood in front of it and said. "I hear you wanted to see me". She reared back in her chair with this evil looking smirk on her face. The exact same look that I remember seeing on Grace's face. Remembering that these two Administrative Officers were and still are good friends. I then wondered if possibly they both might have attended the same hate thy employee school.

She then said, "Mr. Johnson, because of your so called disability and your inability to perform your duties satisfactory. I find it necessary to remove you from your job as Accounting Technician and place you in the mail room to open mail and answer the phones". "Bang! Boom! Ring! Flash!" A total outrageous for of rage hit melike a bolt of lightning. Everything went totally black! The next thing I remembered was waking up in an ambulance on the way to the hospital. I had an IV line in my arm and an oxygen mask over my face. Totally oblivious as to what happened. From what I could gather, from the paramedics, I tried to attack Mazoo and passed out in the process. Then they said we think you've had a heart attack. They proceeded to ask me what led up to this incident.

I tried to explain what I remembered of that moment, but found it hard to concentrate. I do remember telling them of the horrible treatment that I have endured in the past two years at the hands of the Federal Government. Then to add insult to injury, one of the paramedics told me that the woman I tried to attack told him to tell me, "Make sure Mr. Johnson brings me a doctor's slip tomorrow, when he returns to work".

Well with God as my witness, June 14, 1994 was my last day of word with the United Stated Department of Agriculture and anyone else for that matter.

I spent the next two days in the hospital undergoing many tests to determine what damage if any was done to my heart. The tests revealed that I got so upset that I had what they call a mild cardiac infarction, which was brought on by an extreme provoked anxiety attack.

The doctors made it very clear that I was not to return to that stressful job that caused this provoked anxiety attack. They also told me that I was a very lucky guy. If it were not for the fact that I was in such good shape, this incident could have been fatal. The doctor also recommended that I continue my Psychotherapy treatments and continue taking my medication.

After I was released from the hospital I went home and called Dr. Lilly and told her what had just happened. Of course she was totally shocked and concerned. She told me she wanted to see me as soon as possible and for me not to try to drive myself. I told her that I had a very good friend who could drove me to her office, the next afternoon.

I Fought the Law and I Won

So on this day I started what was to be a regular BI-monthly therapy sessions that would last the rest of my life.

Dr. Lilly had called my attorney and told him what happened. Once my attorney found out what happened, he immediately called me and told me to file a Worker's Compensation Claim against the United Stated Department of Agriculture and under no circumstances was I to return to work. At this time he also submitted EEO Grievance number seven (7) for violation of American's with Disabilities Act, and falsifying Government documents.

It took me several days at home before I was able to resume some sort of life because, of what was later to be diagnosed as Major Depressive Disorder and Extreme Anxiety Attacks.

I filed the Worker's Compensation claim for these above disorders.

Before the Worker's compensation claim was granted, I had to use up all my sick leave and annual leave. During this time Mazoo kept up her harassments towards me, as if I were still her employee. She hounded me weekly, with tons of paper works to fill out, doctor's letters to be sent in, medical forms to fill out and so on and so on. Seems that once she finally realized I wasn't coming back and that I had filed charges against her, she became obsessed with making my life a pure hell. She even went so far as to try and sabotage my Workers Compensation Claim by filing false statements of which she later recanted when caught. It was if she was obsessed with making my life as miserable as she could. It got to the point where I had to have my attorney correspond with her, as she made me too upset.

When this latest EEO grievance reached the administrative level. I once again had to appear at a Dispute and Resolution Board hearing where the facts of this case were presented. My attorney made it very clear to the Chairman of the board that under no circumstances was I to be in the same room with my former supervisor, Mazoo. He made it very clear that the presence of this woman would aggravate my already delicate mental condition. But much to our surprise she did appear. The minute she appeared at the office door, the hard on the back of my neck stood up on end. I starting breathing real hard, my heart was racing so fast, I thought it was going to burst. Everyone in the room could obviously see my reaction to her presence. My attorney immediately stood up and screamed. "That woman is not supposed to be in this room"!

The Chairman of the board immediately turned to Mazoo and said "You leave this hearing at once".

Almost looking like she was upset, she looked straight at me with that awful grin and said, "I have no problem with leaving. Then she turned and left.

During this hearing it was established at management did indeed violate the Americans With Disability Act (ADA), by placing me in a position that was obvious beyond my physical ability. It was also established that my Supervisor, Mazoo was indeed a close friend of my former supervisor, Grace, who was also found guilty at a previous administrative hearing and transferred to another location. The board concluded that Mazoo's defense of my improprieties in my job were false and had no merit.

The board also said, "all her claims were found improper and unfounded, because she used a subordinate employee to relay gossip, which was used to substantiate her accusations".

For this EEO Grievance, my attorney and I agreed to a quick settlement. It was obvious that we had beaten them at their own game and it would serve no purpose to carry this incident any further. It was more important that we focus our attentions on the previous and most damaging cases that were still pending.

Management agreed that if at such a time, as my psychiatrist felt I could resume employment that I would return to a position of equal grade if not higher. I would also receive all back annual leave and sick leave that I used after I left the agency. I would also receive an undisclosed amount of money for compensatory damages.

A couple of days after this hearing I heard through reliable sources that Mazoo was removed from her position as Administrative Officer and re-assigned to another undisclosed location.

In the meantime the other EEO claims, that we rejected by the DRB had run their administrative courses and were not resolved at that level. Because the USDA could not resolve these claims to our satisfaction and we had exhausted all administrative remedies possible by law, we then filed suit in Federal Court.

On November 16, 1995 we filed suit in The United States District Court for the District of Columbia, against Daniel Glickman, in his capacity as Secretary of the United States Department of Agriculture.

Charges being: that as a result of the wrongful acts of and to include, discrimination by the defendant, the plaintiff has been injured in his health, sustaining physical and mental injury to his body and nervous system. Such injuries having caused and will, in a reasonable probability continue to cause the plaintiff great mental anguish, physical pain and suffering humiliation, shock and injury to his reputation. That, in committing the foregoing wrongful acts, the Secretary, acting through agents and vice-principals, failed to remedy past discrimination and continues to support, conduct and enforce invidious discrimination based on, inter alia, sex, age and handicap status.

The defendant acted in an intentional, reckless and/or callous disregard for the Constitution and Statutory Rights of the Plaintiff.

After a month or so, management came back with another offer of settlement, of which we rejected. By rejecting their offers this gave us the upper hand to force this very delicate discrimination issue into the Federal Courts, where the whole world could see how the U.S. Government treats its employees.

Then Judge Thomas Pinfield Jackson ordered that this case go before a mediator. In doing this the Judge appoints an unbiased third party to mediate this issue, which gives management a chance to save face and eliminate a possible trial in Federal Court. A trial in Federal Court is just what we wanted, but it was what management wanted to avoid.

If this case had ever gone to trial, heads all over the USDA would have rolled.

The first mediation hearing was a joke. The mediator was an Employee Relations Specialist from a large firm located in Washington DC. The mediation hearing broke down when management again refused to meet our requests. The case then went back to Judge Jackson.

On Oct. 8, 1996, Judge Thomas Pinfield Jackson ordered this case back to mediation and also ordered that someone of settlement authority attend from the USDA. He ordered that this mediation be held no later than December 2, 1996.

The next mediation hearing was held on December 1, 1996 to no avail. Management still playing the "we did nothing wrong scenario" gave in on more of our demands, but was deadlocked on the amount of Compensatory Damages.

I had to be removed from the room when I got very emotional over the portion when the government tried to down play the sexual remark made by my supervisor. I felt the same feeling coming over me that I felt the day I had my heart attack at work.

After regaining my composure in an adjacent room, the mediator came in and tried to smooth things over. I jumped up! My attorney grabbed my coat, trying to hold me back, I stated, "How would you like it if your supervisor called you a "Blacked Dyke"? She went white! After she regained her composure, shut her mouth, she silently left the room. My attorney told me to stay seated and he left the room and went back to the mediation meeting room. He was gone about 15 minutes, when he returned, he said, "They upped the amount".

At this point I was so upset with their total disregard for my Civil rights that I refused every offer they presented. I recited from Federal Law the definition of what Civil Rights was. I also told them that as far as I was concerned this case would go to a jury and the Press! When I said press, they got worried. I told them all this meeting was over.

So with this meeting ending with no resolution, this meant that it went back to the Judge again.

After my Attorney the court that there was still no settlement, the Judge made his last and final order. Sometimes at the end of February or the beginning of March 1997. Judge Jackson ordered yet another mediation meeting and sternly ordered the Government to settle this matter immediately or he would!

With this aggressive order from the Judge, management knew what the maximum compensatory damages could be awarded if we went to court and they decided to settle.

On July 3, 1997 both parties signed a stipulation for compromise settlement for an undisclosed amount. I was told, as of this date this was the largest amount ever awarded to a single individual, on Violation of Civil Rights. This did not include the legal fees, they were paid separate.

Thinking that all my troubles with the Federal Government were behind me, well not so fast. The Government was not finished with me yet. There are still mighty deep waters to tread!

Remembering I had filed two (2) applications with The Federal Workers Compensation board of which they both were accepted. The first one stemming from the detail to the warehouse, for aggravation of Severe Carpal Tunnel Syndrome. The second stemming from the infamous memo where I was called, "A Flaming Queer", this being for Major Depression Disorder. Since the law does not allow you to be compensated for two claims, they combined the two claims into one.

When I filed the applications for Workers Compensation in 1994, I also called the USDA Personnel Office to see what I had to do to apply for Disability Retirement. I knew that after all I had just been through, with the thought of being dependent on depression medication for the rest of my life, I needed to apply for disability retirement.

When I called Personnel I spoke with a retirement Personnel Specialist a GS-12, who informed me that because I was being paid a monthly salary by Workers Compensation, I did not have to file for Disability Retirement until I was removed from Workers Compensation. Taking this information as being true I forgot about the USDA Retirement.

I now centered my attentions on applying for Social Security Disability. This process in itself is a nightmare. I filed my claim in January of 1996. This first claim was denied. I immediately appealed this decision in May of 1996. Again they denied my claim. At this point I was really getting pretty upset. The final stage of appeal was when you request to have an oral hearing in front of an Administrative Law Judge.

On November 8, 1996 I requested this hearing, at which time I had to retain the legal assistance of an Attorney who specialized in Social Security Disability cases. I received a letter from Social Security that my hearing was scheduled for August 12, 1997. With well-documented evidence from my Psychiatrist, the EEO Discrimination Cases along with the Settlement Agreement made by the Government, Mr. Jacoby presented a most argumentative case in my defense. The only bad part about this hearing was the grueling questions I had to answer. There was a Law Judge and a licensed Physician present. Between the two of them they really raked me over the coals. With all the antidepressant drugs that I had to take, I couldn't even drive myself to this hearing. Mr. Jacoby had to pick me up and drive me to downtown DC. With the hearing being at 8:30 AM I could hardly keep my eyes open.

On August 16, 1997, I was awarded full benefits from Social Security. A hint to anyone who applies for Social Security Disability. The Social Security Administration denies every claim for disability twice, automatically whether you are totally disabled or not, they will deny you. Don't give up; request those two (2) Appeals, then make that last ditch effort and go in front of the Administrative Judge. This is when you will win. It is another tragic miscarriage of justice by our Government knowing full well that you have paid into Social Security your entire life and when you need it the most, they make you jump through fire before they give it to you. They try to wear you down mentally with all the appeals, in hopes you will give up before you

I Fought the Law and I Won

finally get it. Then there is the chance that after all this; you still may not receive your benefits.

By this point I am receiving both compensation from Workers Compensation along with Social Security Disability. I will have to continue seeing my Psychiatrist twice a month for the rest of my life. I am taking Elavil, Lithium and Zoloft for depression. Xanax for anxiety attacks and Ambien to sleep. No matter how many different drugs I have to take, I still have those horrifying nightmares.

By now I feel that my life has come to this point where I have to take medication to get up, take medication to maintain during the day and more medication to go to sleep at night.

If I thought my problems were over, well think again. The government throws another monkey wrench into the works.

Dr. Lilly will have to send in her reports on a regular basis whenever the Office of Workers Compensation asks for them. When the Office of Workers Compensation feels if my doctor is not sending the proper reports to sustain my claim, under the Worker's Compensation Act they have the right to send me to another doctor of their choosing. I went to see a couple of different Psychiatrist's or their version of what they call a Psychiatrist on several occasions.

This one particular Psychiatrist that they sent me to was a real trip in itself. I arrived at his office 20 minutes early, as not to be late. There was no receptionist in the office. I sat in one of two chairs for over an hour. No magazines to read, no pictures on the wall, not even so much of an artificial plant. Just when I was getting ready to leave, I saw a person come in the back door secretly, not even looking to see if anyone was in the office.

I waited for another fifteen (15) minutes before he came to the door and said, "Are you ready"? I replied, "I've been waiting for an hour and fifteen (15) minutes, I guess I am ready". I was escorted to what was supposed to be his examining office. There was a so-called desk that had papers piled five (5) feet high on it. A window that looked directly into the waiting room of another Doctors office, where those patients could look in he and I and vice versa. Of course there was no curtains on these windows to close. There were two chairs in this office. He sat in one and I sat in the other. He pulled his chair right up in front of me, not even three feet between us. The first word that came out of his mouth was liked to have a knocked me out. He reeked of Booze: I mean a lot of Booze. This doctor was stewed to the gills.

I spent approximately 20 minutes in from of this horrible smelling individual. He did nothing but ask me a million questions about everything in my life from the day I was born to did I ever have sex with my mother. After this horrifying exam. I couldn't get out of his office fast enough. Before I left he informed me that he would have these notes typed up and a report sent to Worker's Compensation.

It took about two weeks for his two-page report to reach Worker's Compensation. It only took Worker's Compensation two days deliver their blows. It seems that this alcoholic, perverted doctor wrote in his report just what OWCP wanted to read in order to deny my claim.

Workers Compensation sent me the most disturbing news yet. They were denying my claim and cutting off all my benefits. This included my monthly check and medical benefits.

Of course they said I could appeal this decision, of which I immediately did. Again the government goes to work on your head trying to break you down and make you give up. At this point I had nothing to lose and since I had come this far I was not going for anything less than the best. I appealed once, they denied it. I appealed that appeal and again they denied that appeal. Just like Social Security you have that last ditched effort to appear in front of an Administrative Law Judge to plead for your life. I requested this hearing and it was granted for November 1, 1998.

My attorney again argued with a great defense. This time it was in front of three Administrative Law Judges. My defense being documents from outside doctors and the ultimate win of six EEO cases. He also used the documentation of the abuse I received while employed at the USDA.

I Fought the Law and I Won

On December 23, 1998, on my 50th Birthday I received the best birthday present possible. The Administrative Law Judges decision to reverse the denial from OWCP. They granted me, all back compensatory damages, future compensatory benefits, all Medical and life Insurance benefits restored. Though this was a great triumph for me, I wasn't out of the woods yet.

Under the Worker's Compensation Act, it stated that I had to undergo yet another psychiatric evaluation. This time it was going to be a much more extensive and technical evaluation. OWCP arranged three different examinations for me with one well-known prominent Psychiatrist and his assistant a Psychologist. Over the next two weeks I had three different appointments with these two doctors.

The first appointment was a two-hour evaluation with the Psychiatrist. We basically sat around his desk and talked about my past. He was a much more thorough and compassionate Psychiatrist then any of the others that OWCP had me see. I really felt comfortable being with this doctor. During this evaluation he ask that the next time I met with him, that I furnish him with all the legal documentation that I had involving my EEO cases, and subsequent decisions and damages awarded. I informed him that some of the documents that he was requesting were confidential and were not be viewed by anyone else. He assured me that he would not reveal any specific details contained in these documents, just use the information contained in them to substantiate his diagnosis. With this I felt confident to release this information to him.

My second appointment was with this prominent Psychologist whom was another part of this network of psychiatric doctors. I spent four grueling hours with this doctor. He put me through more tests then I had ever taken in my whole life. Many of the tests were in writing and many others were oral. What were to seem like the never-ending tests, there at the end were the infamous Inkblots? I have heard all my life of people taking this test and what strange outcome people have experienced with them. I now know why they call them strange. Every time he would flash one of them at me, I said what it looked like to me. He then said, "are you sure it looks like that"? I said, "Yes, you ask me what I thought it looked like and I told you! Then he'd flash another one.

I again told him what I thought it looked like. He repeated again, "Are you sure"? I repeated again, "yes I am sure, why do you keep asking me if I am sure"? This went on through the entire stack of inkblot cards. After this very uneventful test I felt as if I had just flunked a final exam in college. I was so glad when he said that this portion of the test was over.

My third and final appointment was with the Psychiatrist again. At this appointment I brought him a hardbound folder approximately six inches thick of documents from A to Z on my horrific experiences with the USDA. I again reminded him that most of these documents were confidential Government documents and not for public viewing. He assured me that this information would stay confidential and he would only read them to obtain information for his final report to OWCP.

He had his secretary makes copies and he returned the originals to me. I spent about two-hours at this last and final visit.

He basically was reading over the documents and asking me questions about my treatment while employed at the USDA. We covered every gory detail that I experienced during the two years at the USDA. It was very hard on me to relieve those awful days and I broke down and cried several times.

After this final visit, he informed me that he and his associate would get together and prepare a final report and submit it to OWCP.

It seems that this part of the nightmare took forever, not knowing what these two doctors were going to say which sealed my fate for the rest of my life.

While waiting for this report and knowing the Government like I do, I was expecting the worst.

I remembered what the Personnel Specialist at USDA had earlier told me: As long as you are on OWCP rolls you don't have to file for USDA disability Retirement. So with this thought in mind I called the USDA Personnel Office and voiced my concerns about my OWCP status. Just in case this last medical report did not go in my favor and my claim was denied again, I wanted to have this ace in the hole. So I ask them to send me the necessary forms to fill out for Disability Retirement.

They sent me an application for USDA Disability Retirement. I filled out this application and returned it to the appropriate office.

On April 15, 1999, the final report was written by the two doctors at the Metropolitan Psychiatric Group and sent to OWCP. My attorney and I tried for two weeks to get a copy of the report, of which we finally received. Much to our surprise the report was seventeen pages long. The final diagnosis being: "On the basis of my assessment with Mr. Johnson, clinically it is clear that there has been an ongoing conflictual relationship between the claimant and the Department of Agriculture, as exemplified by his repeated EEO complaints which have largely been substantiated. It is evident that he has felt victimized and some degree this has been confirmed by the outcome of his EEO complaints, but these are not considered to be factors of employment for the purpose of this analysis,"

"Hence, in considering the issues relevant to this examination one must only focus on the highlighted fact of the finding of Mr. Johnson receiving an office memorandum describing him in negative and prejudicial sexual terms".

"Further, while there is evidence of a residual work related condition, namely a Severe Major Depressive Disorder. However, it is evident that the degree of conflict between he and the USDA would make his return to employment virtually impossible and likely to result in significant regression and hostilities".

"On the basis of his current presentation I would conclude that returning to employment is highly unlikely, because of the personality disorder".

With this report, the Office of Federal Worker's Compensation has placed on me, "Total Disability", with all benefits included.

Needless to say this news was the best news of my life. At least for the time being. Knowing what I know today about the Government I will always be looking over my shoulder for yet another regulation or law for them to try and break.

Low and behold the Government still had one more monkey wrench to throw at me, this being the biggest one yet!

Now let's go back a page or two, to where I filed the application with the USDA for retirement disability. This being the Disability Retirement that I earned and deserved as an employee of the USDA.

Remembering also the information that I received from the USDA Personnel Specialist, who stated, "You don't have to file for retirement disability while you are still on the OWCP rolls"! Well she was WRONG!

This miss-guided information from a 20-year veteran of the USDA's Personnel Office would turn out to be the biggest challenge yet for me, in trying to collect my due disability.

My application was returned to me from the Office of Personnel Management (OPM) with this reply! "Your application for retirement disability has been returned to you because you failed to file for disability retirement within the one year separation date which is mandated by Congress. Well to say this hit me like a wrecking ball would be putting it mildly. I once again placed my lifeline of Disability Retirement in what I thought was competent hands.

After regaining my composure and facing reality, I said to myself, "This shouldn't surprise me, after what I have just been through and knowing the Government like I do, I have yet another chapter to add to this never ending fight".

First and foremost I immediately call the Person at the USDA's Personnel Office that gave me this incorrect information. I explained to her that I filed the original application for Retirement Disability with her on February 2, 1996. I then reminded her that she sent the application back to me with the following explanation: "You don't have to file for Disability Retirement while you are on the OWCP rolls. She replied, "That's right"!

I then told her that I had sent another application to OPM for processing on November 6, 1996.

I further told her that OPM has returned that application with the following explanation: "Mr. Johnson you were separated from Federal Service on May 29, 1995 and your application for Retirement Disability was filed at this office on November 6, 1996. This application does not fall within the mandated law of one year from separation. Your application is thus for denied"!

Being totally speechless the Personnel Specialist replied, "I am so sorry Mr. Johnson, I thought that as long as you were on the OWCP rolls, that you didn't have to file for Disability Retirement", I replied, "How could you give me this false information that now jeopardizes my retirement"? All she could do was apologize and apologize over and over. I knew then that this was going to be the greatest challenge of all.

I spoke with OPM specialists, OPM supervisors, and every legal person at my disposal. Everyone says that same thing? The law is strict and binding pertaining to this one-year separation policy, and the only relief possible is to take OPM to court or file a complaint with the Merit Systems Protection Board. My defense of receiving false information from a Personnel Specialist that deals with disability retirement fell on deaf ears.

After doing a great deal of searching and digging though Federal Laws and Regulations I came to the conclusion that there were two separate avenues to take in trying to resolve this last and final chapter in my life. It never seemed to let up. Every time I took one step forward, I got knocked back two.

The first course of action was to file an appeal with the Merit Systems Protection Board. (MSPB) This board is made up of administrative Law Judges that act like the watchdogs over Federal Employees right.

The second course of action is if the MSPB denies your appeal, you can file civil charges against the Office of Personnel Management (OPM), in the Federal Court of Appeals.

I filed the appeal with the Merit Systems Protection Board (MSPB).

Having already spent the past 4 years in Administrative hearings, Criminal mediation hearings, and Federal Court hearings and with mountains of paper work and no legal assistance from an attorney. I decide to go this one alone. I represented myself.

On June 23, 1997, I filed an Appeal with the United States of America Merit Systems Protection Board in the Washington DC Regional Office. My argument being that the USDA Personnel Office misrepresented me when applying for Retirement Disability. I was given false information when attempting to file for Disability. I submitted as evidence the original application filed on February 2, 1996. I also submitted the second application that I filed with OPM on November 6, 1996. My defense being, my separation date of May 29, 1995 and my first application for disability on February 2, 1996 did fall within the OPM guidelines of one year.

This clearly shows that I did attempt to file within the guidelines but this application was retuned, reason being I need not apply for Disability Retirement while still on the OWCP rolls.

On July 30, 1997, the Administrative Law Judge from MSPB ordered that there be a telephonic prehearing conference on thephone with the Administrative Law Judge, myself, the U.S. Assistant Attorney assigned to this case and Ms. Jackson, the Personnel Specialist who gave me the false information.

The conference hearing was scheduled for August 15, 1997 at 9:30AM.

The morning of August 15, 1997 was a very nervous and stressful time for me as I awaited the fateful call from the Judges Office. At exactly 9:30AM the phone rang. It was Judge Smith on the line. Her first words were, "This is teleconference, being recorded in the case

I Fought the Law and I Won

of Charles F. Johnson vs. Office of Personnel Management, Docket Number PH-0845-97-0328-I-1.

She then asks if The U.S. Attorney was on the line. He said, "Yes Your Honor I'm here". Judge Smith then ask if Ms. Jackson, the Personnel specialist was on the line. She said, "Yes Your Honor I'm here". The Judge then ordered all parties to raise their right hand. I raised my right hand. The Judge then said, "Do you and all of you on this telephonic conference swear to tell the truth, the whole truth and nothing but the truth, so help you God"? All three of us at the same time said "I do". The Judge having everyone sworn in, laid out the format for this conference. She said, "Mr. Johnson you will present your case and if need be, you can ask Ms. Jackson any questions you like. Then the U.S. District Attorney can present his case and ask either of you any questions of he needs to".

Without actually reading the complete teleconference word for word, which lasted a total of 30 minutes in all. I will give a rough translation of what was said. I initially gave the same testimony as I had given in the previous filed documents. My defense being that I was given false information pertaining to my attempt to apply to apple for Federal Disability Retirement. My main objective at this point was to get on tape the documented testimony from Ms. Jackson admitting that she had indeed given me false information when I applied to her office for Disability Retirement.

During this portion of the recording I specifically addressed Ms. Jackson with this question. "Ms. Jackson did you not return my first application for Retirement Disability, dated February 2, 1996"? She replied, "Yes I did".

I then ask her. "Ms. Jackson did you not tell me that the reason you were returning the application was that I didn't have to file for Disability Retirement while I was still on the OWCP rolls"? She replied. "Yes I did". I then said "Ms. Jackson how long have you been a Personnel Specialist dealing with Disability Retirements"? She replied. "Approximately 20 years". My last question to her was, Ms. Jackson. "Why did you give me that false information"? She replied, "I was always under the impression that as long as an employee was on the OWCP rolls, they did not have to apply for disability retirement". I said, "Thank you Ms. Jackson I have no further questions for you".

Judge Smith then said, "Ms. Jackson is it your sworn testimony that you, not maliciously, told Mr. Johnson that he did not have to file for Disability Retirement because he was still on the OWCP rolls"? She replied, "That is what I was made to believe. "Yes".

Judge Smith then ask if the U.S Attorney had any questions for either of us. He replied, "No Your Honor I do not". Judge Smith then announced that the teleconference was over. She said, "I am now terminating the recorded portion of this conference". Judge Smith thanked the U.S. Attorney, Ms. Jackson and myself for our co-operation in this matter. Judge Smith said, "Mr. Johnson you will get my decision within the next few weeks". She then hung up. Boy my palms were sweaty and my heart was racing to beat the band. I felt like I had just run a 20-mile marathon.

On October 2, 1997 I received the Initial Decision from Judge Smith. It read:

"The appellant appealed to the Office of Personnel Management's (OPM'S) reconsideration decision, denying his application for Disability Retirement under the Federal Employee's Retirement System (FERS) as untimely filed after the statutory one year time limit. The Board has jurisdiction over this appeal under 5 U.S.C. 8461(e)(l); 5 C.F.R. 841.308. For the following reasons, the agency's, decision is AFFIRMED".

Well, to say this was a great blow to my future, would be the understatement of the year. Thinking for sure that with Ms. Jackson's testimony it would go in my favor. In the Judge's decision, she went strictly, by the book. No matter if I was given false information or not, the law still holds true on the one year statute.

Although in her decision letter the Judge said, "That if I did not agree with her decision, I could file a petition for review". Of course, that is just what I did. Knowing good and well I was wasting my time, but right from the beginning, I have always exhausted every and all avenues of jurisprudence before giving up.

I filed the request for review, but other than taking up time and wasting Government paperwork her decision was upheld in its final stages. This final decision left still yet another appeal. This next step or Appeal was to the United States Federal Court of Appeals.

On March 20, 1998, I filed notice of submission without oral argument to the United States Federal Court of Appeals for the Federal Circuit, case number 98-3110 Johnson vs. OPM.

I received a letter from the Appeals Court notifying me that the above case will be submitted to a panel of three Judges of the court on June 1, 1998. The panel will decide the appeal on the briefs without oral argument.

I did my homework and had the option of appearing in front of the court or have them decide the merits from my brief filed with the court. With my mental state being the way that it was and the amount of medication that I was taking, there was no way I could appear in person to argue this appeal. Besides, I knew what the outcome was going to be before I submitted my 50 page brief. I argued my fool head off. I hit them with everything but the kitchen sink. I usedevery page of defense that I had: including my six successfully won EEO cases.

Of course now that I have taken this case one more step up the ladder of Justice, the U.S. Assistant District Attorney had to file his arguments too. Well this case took a bit longer than any of us had expected. Seems the U.S. Attorney's Office was short of Assistant's to file the brief on behalf of the U.S. government. The U.S. Attorney's office sent the Appeals Court three motions for Enlargement of Time of which the court granted. What this means is that the Assistant Attorney's Office changed three different times the person that was to represent the U.S. Government. The U.S. Attorney's office did finally choose an Assistant U.S. Attorney to represent the Office of Personnel Management.

After a ton of paper work, three requests of Enlargement of Time, three different U.S. Assistant Attorney's and three different sets of briefs, the Court of Appeals finally heard my case.

On June 5, 1998, the United States court of Appeals for the Federal Circuit case No. 98-3110, Charles F. Johnson (petitioner) V. Office of Personnel Management (Respondent) made its Judgment. After all this time and the anxiety attacks that I suffered during this most stressful case, the Order read as a single word typed right in the middle of the page, "AFFIRMED". Which meant another victory for the Government and supposedly another defeat for me.

Of course now, let's not give up hope so quickly. In their decision they offer yet another ray of hope, being, none other then the United States Supreme Court.

WOW! Me having a case heard in front of the highest Court in the land. No this had to be a dream or at most a horrible nightmare. My case going to the ultimate Jurist of the land.

Why not? What do I have to lose? Yes, I went for it, the big one!

In order to begin to think about filing an appeal with the United States Supreme Court, there are many, many, hoops one must jump through just to file a case.

Fortunately I live right outside the District of Columbia in Maryland. That makes it a local call for me. Just imagine being able to just pick up the phone and dial ten digits and get to talk to someone at the U.S. Supreme Court. Well that's just what I did. I reached one of many clerks of the court, a man we will call Mr. Suter. I explained to Mr. Suter my situation and I wanted to file an Appeal with the United States Supreme Court. Of course I was waiting for him to laugh in my ear, but to the contrary he was very nice and polite.

He explained to me that there are very strict guidelines and rules to follow in order just to get your case accepted and placed on the court docket. So, I ask him if he would please send me the necessary

I Fought the Law and I Won

materials that I needed to file an appeal? He asked for my name and address of which I excitedly stuttered to him. He then told me to read the entire booklet on the Rules of the Supreme Court. Then he said, "Follow all the instructions on the 15 page application". He then jokingly said, "It's obvious you are not an attorney"? I jokingly replied, "You can tell"? With this we had established a friendly rapport. He then said, "You are going to file this appeal by yourself"? I replied, "Yes is that legal"? With a great big laugh he then said, "Yes it's legal, but very unusual". He then said, "There is a $300.00 filing fee". I chocked back and said, "300.00? I can't afford that".

Then to my relief, he informed me that people that file appeals on their own and don't have the resources to pay this fee, they can make a request to the court for a motion for leave to Proceed in Forma Pauper is. This is a request to the court to waive this fee because you do not have the available funds to cover this fee.

I explained to him that I was a disabled Veteran, who at this time was living on Social Security Disability. He replied, "You most definitely can file In Forma Pauper is. I'll include an application for this in the package I am going to send you". I thanked him with all my heart for his assistance. He said if I had any problems with the answering of any questions or if I had any problems completing the forms, just call and ask for him and he would be more than happy to assist me. Now I ask you, "is that not the voice of a saint"?

He was one of the very few Federal employees that you will ever meet in this lifetime that will make you feel proud to be an American.

Approximately a week later I received this very large envelope from The United States Supreme Court. The mailman ever brought it to my door and handed it to me personally and said, "Boy Mr. Johnson you must have really gone and done something big this time"!

I jokingly laughed and said, "Yep, I sure did".

In this envelope from the Supreme Court were approximately 25 pages of forms to fill out. The most important one, the request to file In Forma Pauper is. This one was the first one that I filled out. It basically was a questionnaire about my financial status. Then I proceeded with the long and tedious process of filling out the rest of the forms.

Man! It sure takes a lot of time and there were, it seemed like, a million questions to answer. It took me about three days in all to complete the while package. I then signed everything and placed it in the largest envelope I could find and took it to the Post Office to mail. I couldn't believe how heavy this envelope was. It took $3.25 worth of postage just to send it regular mail.

On September 24, 1998 my case was filed with the United States Supreme Court.

On October 5, 1998 I received a letter from The Clerk of the Court, Mr. Suter informing me that my case had been received, my request to proceed In Forma Pauper is was granted and my case placed on the docket for October 2, 1998 as No. 98-6272.

On October 27, 1998 I received a waiver from the U.S. Solicitor General's Office where they were waiving their right to file a response to my Petition. This means the U.S. Attorney for OPM would not be making any responses to my application for appealing the lower court decision.

Of course this part of the Supreme Court filing is the easiest. The blood, sweat and tears are just beginning. With all the cases that the Supreme Court receives, and the short time that they are actually in session, a panel of Judges reviews all cases in order to streamline the actual cases that they get presented to the complete Supreme Court Judges.

So the waiting process begins. Of course just having a case that is accepted and placed on the docket is a monumental feat in itself. Thousands of cases never get this far. I am still optimistic though, figuring that someone up there sees the mighty injustice that has been done to me and will at least listen.

The bad news didn't take as long as I had expected.

I Fought the Law and I Won

On November 1, 1998 the Supreme Court decided not to hear my case and AFFIRMED the lower court decision.

BUT! There is still a faint light at the end of the tunnel.

One of the Justice had made a very unusual and remarkable statement, which later was to be a landmark award recommendation.

He said, "This case has potential merit for the fact that a misrepresentation was made in a most discriminating manner", "BINGO" the magic word, "Discrimination". Of course, what have I been doing for the past four years? My brain was so abused and highly medicated that I had forgotten the original scope of my filings of all the EEO discrimination grievances. How could be I be so blind, trying to resolve this matter using the wrong approach?

So again I filed yet another and my final EEO Grievance against the United States Department of Agriculture: for violation of the Americans with Disability Act (ADA).

This was to be the easiest and fastest one so far and with the largest award ever. Even topping my original settlement.

I called the office of Civil Rights Administration at the United States Department of Agriculture. Much to my surprise the procedures for filing EEO grievance had changed since the last time I had filed one. It seems as if you didn't have to go through all the red tape that you used to. Because of the magnitude of cases that were backlogged on their files, they had streamlined the process for filing.

I was forwarded to a Civil Rights counselor of whom we will call Harry.

Harry came on the line and introduced himself to me and asks, "What it was that he could help me with"? I return introduced myself to him and said, "I wanted to file an informal EEO grievance against the agency.

I started off by giving Harry some background information on my previous dealings with the agency and the six other EEO grievances that I had filed previously. He was quite interested in the details of the other cases that I had won. I tied to be as brief as possible without going into too graphic a detail. But since he was supposed to be the Specialist in charge of filing this new case, he needed to have much more of the details on the previous cases.

Without sounding like the conqueror that I was, I highlighted the most important aspects of the cases. I suppose we were on the phone for about an hour total. Seems as though the more I talked, the more he listened. The more he listened the more curious he got. He said, "In his 12 year career as a Civil Rights Counselor he had not heard of such cases as I just told him about."

I then proceeded to tell him about the incident with the Personnel Office and the fact that I was given false information pertaining to my applying for disability retirement. I also told him that the Office of Personnel Management denied my claim for disability retirement because of the untimely filing. The reason for the untimely filing was due to the fact that I received false information from a Personnel Specialist at the USDA.

I then told him that I appealed OPM's denial by filing an appeal with the Merit System Protection Board. Of course at this point I had him sitting on the edge of his chair. He said, "Go On"! I then told him that I had a three-way teleconference with an Administrative Law Judge.

I couldn't believe how fascinated he was with my tales of woe.

At this point I figured that I had kept this man much too long on the phone and I was getting a bit tired myself, so I suggested that he fax me all the information I needed to file this grievance. He told me how sorry he was that I had been put through all this torment. I thanked him very much for his concerns and said, "I'll anxiously await your fax".

I guess it was around 2:30PM when we ended the conversation and low and behold I receive a fax within ten minutes, from Harry. Attached to the form letter for filing an EEO grievance was a note saying, "I'll call you tomorrow and we can continue our conversation".

The next day, sure enough Harry called, with his professional and outgoing personality; he wanted to know if I had read over the format for filing an EEO grievance and I said, "Yes I did".

Of course he then said, "I know there are going to be questions". I said. "Why of course, you did not think I was going to let you off that easy, did you"? He chuckled and said, "Through it all you still manage to have a sense of humor". I replied, "Yes they stripped me of my career, my personality, my mental stability, my freedom of being around people, but they didn't get my sense of humor", we discussed briefly some more of the specifies of the other cases I had filed. He kept saying he wanted to get a bigger and better picture of just what has happened up to this point.

I informed him that from the DRB I appealed it to the Federal Court of Appeals and then right on up to the United States Supreme Court. I told him I've hit them all with everything I had. Finally at the Supreme Courts door I got the best and final word on the fate of my future.

So I sat down and drafted a rough sketch of what I wanted to put in this final and last EEO grievance.

I wrote down that I felt that I was discriminated against by a Personnel Specialist whose job it is to know whether or not a Workers Compensation Claim is grounds for denying retirement disability. I felt that under the Federal with Disabilities Act of 1994, I was denied disability retirement by no fault of mine.

After reading and re-reading this over and over, I figured that there were only so many ways to approach this problem, and I just about covered them all. I wanted to be extra sure that I worded this grievance properly so they wouldn't have any new ammunition to use to get it denied on some technicality.

After talking back and forth with Harry a few times he got to know basically what I was trying to say.

We just had to make sure we had all our I's dotted and T's crossed.

I faxed the final draft of just what I wanted to say and of course along with the grounds for filing an EEO grievance you have to include the compensatory damages. It was the compensatory damages that held up my former grievances so long, so I wanted to be sure this time to get it right.

Once Harry read the final draft he called me and said, "Mr. Johnson you seem to have everything in order and it sure looks as though you have done this before". But there is one problem? Well I knew it was too good to be true, everything was going too smooth. So I said, "What problem"?

Harry said, "There is no dispute about your disability and the fact that you were successful in your previous EEO cases, but where is the evidence to prove neglect on the part of the agency in this matter"?

I had to think this one over for a few minutes, as by this time my thoughts were getting very mixed up. In the past I would have fired off the answer in a matter of seconds. But my mind went totally blank, and it definitely scared the hell out of me. I had to tell Harry that I was not feeling well and could he keep that thought in mind and I would get back to him. He asked if I was all right, and I said "No I am not", It was a comfort though knowing that he cared to ask, I told him I would call him back later.

By now it was very obvious to myself and everyone around me, including my psychiatrist that I was headed for a mental breakdown. The tough guy image was about to take a tumble. For the past two years I had endured severe mental anguish, verbal abuse, sexual harassment, sexual discrimination, age discrimination, disability discrimination not to include those many long grueling hearings I had to attend. I think the mind games that the Government had played on me had finally surfaced in its ugly fashion. At this stage I just sat down and I lost it.

I Fought the Law and I Won

I didn't know what was happening to me. I was hot but I had chills, I could think but I could not remember I knew where I was, but didn't know how I got here. It was if my brain had finally just shut down. It was the scariest feeling I had ever experienced in my life.

I sort of remember going into my bedroom and lying across the bed.

I must have dozed off for an hour or so and then I remember the phone ringing. This ringing was the loudest ring I think I have ever heard. I picked up the phone and it was my Psychiatrist. I thought I was dreaming and she was in it. She said, "Mr. Johnson you are all right"?

I said, "Why are you calling me, and what time is it"? She said, "Mr. Johnson, a Mr. Green from the USA Civil Rights Division called me and told me he thought you needed help. Mr. Green told me he was talking to you on the phone and you became very mentally unstable and you had to hang up because you weren't feeling good. She asks again, "Mr. Johnson are you all right"? I said, "I don't know, everything is so fuzzy and I don't seem to know where I am". She then said, "Mr. Johnson can you get to the door and open it up for the paramedics"? I said, "Yes I think so"

Well the next thing I remember was waking up at the hospital and seeing all these different people standing around me. I was hooked up to all sorts of monitors and IV's. I seem to be able to talk to them all right, but was confused as to why I was there.

There is a lot of things I don't remember about this incident but from what they tell me I had just had a nervous breakdown. After a week or so of rest and a lot of medication I was starting to regain my faculties again. The doctors said, "That because of the strain and stress that I had been under, all this had finally caught up with my brain and the body's natural defense is to shut it down. I suppose that is why I couldn't remember anything. The doctor told me that I was very lucky guy, that there was no permanent damage to my brain or heart.

After this incident I was placed on stronger antidepressant and anxiety medication. Of course the Doctors wanted me not to do anything that would upset me or trigger another attack. Dr. Lilly and I worked out a very stringent daily program for me to follow while I was at home. I increased my visits to see her from twice a month to three times a month. Of course she was always a phone call away and she made it very clear to me that I was to call her anytime I needed her.

So with this critical evaluation, stronger medications and the fear of another attack. I had to curtail my mental priorities and try not to get upset.

Boy, was that ever a scary situation. I would have never imagined in a million years that something of this nature would bring me down like this. I suppose I had been suppressing these feeling for a long time and it finally caught up with me.

Well, after this little set back, I still had some unfinished business to attend to. With the increase in medication I had no choice but to take a slower pace than I had previously done.

Much to my surprise when I returned home I had a fax on my machine from Harry at the USDA Civil Rights Department. It was at this point that I remembered we did have some unfinished business to tend to. Honestly I did not even remember where we left off in our last correspondence. This fax would remind me though.

Seems as though Harry was refreshing my memory on the filing of an EEO case against the Agency for Violation of the Americans with Disability Act. At this point it was coming back to me, slowly but eventually getting there.

Harry reminded me that, I felt that I was discriminated against by the agency for failing to provide me adequate information when applying for disability retirement.

The problem was that I had to prove that the agency did in deed neglect to give me adequate information while applying for disability retirement. I knew I had the answer to this question right on the tip of my tongue. I was so upset with myself for not being able to bounce right back like I used to do. It seems like everything in my brain was running at half speed. Of course that is exactly what was happening.

So I said to myself, "I know the answer lies in one of the files over in that file cabinet". During the past two years I have documented and amassed a collection of ten, three ring binders filled with all the documents of everything that has taken place in my fight for Civil Rights. I had to just sit down and thumb through these documents and find the answer.

Well luck have it, it only took me thumbing through 3 binders to find the answer to this puzzle.

When I reached the file on the Appeal to the Merit System Protection Board, I ran across the transcripts of the three-way teleconference hearing that took place with the Administrative Law Judge. The MSPB sent me not only the written transcripts of the conference but also an audiocassette tape. In this transcript there is the sworn testimony from Ms. Jackson the Personnel Specialist where she admitted under oath that she did indeed give me false information.

"BINGO" I said, "Harry I have the sworn testimony of the Personnel Specialist who gave me the false information". Harry said, "Do you have this testimony in writing"? I said, "Not only do I have it in writing but I have an audiocassette also".

Harry immediately said, "Mr. Johnson if you have this Personnel Specialist's testimony in writing that she did indeed give you false information while you were applying for disability retirement, that's all I need". Well I was so relieved and elated at the same time.

Harry said, "Mr. Johnson can you fax me a copy of the written transcripts of that hearing"?

I replied, "Of course I will". So I did just that!

With the transcription from the Merit System Protection Board's telephonic conference, where Ms. Jackson admitted giving me false information pertaining to my Disability Retirement, this was all the staff of the Civil Rights office needed to conclude: "The agency failed to accept and process my application for Disability Retirement".

The basis for this informal complaints was the following: Physical Disability, Mental Disability and Reprisal. The Physical and Mental disabilities fall under the Law dealing with Americans with disabilities Act of 1994. The reprisal comes from the obvious intent of the agency to discriminate against me because of my past legal victories against the agency.

Harry took this very important information to his supervisor and explained to her that this was an open and shut case.

Harry called me to give the good news. He said, "My supervisor has given me the authority to offer you a settlement agreement of which you will be compensated for".

Harry said, "Mr. Johnson you know that under this settlement agreement you are awarded compensatory damages". I said, "Yes I know". Harry said, "Mr. Johnson you think it over and let me know what amount you feel you are owed".

How much monetary value do you place on your future and retirement? What documents or calculations do you use to determine how much you will need to substantially provide for your comfortable and disabled economic retirement?

I contacted an investment broker that I know and gave him this problem to solve. After a couple of days to calculate this situation he came up with this solution.

He said, "Mr. Johnson you have to figure out what your original retirement disability monthly pension would have been had you been able to collect it from the first date you applied". That figure is what you want to receive every month for the rest of your life. In order for you to receive this amount every month you must invest in an annuity account that with changing dividend rates will pay you this amount every month.

He came up with this six-figure amount that I would have to invest in an annuity account in order for me to receive this monthly payment for the rest of my life.

After careful consideration and sound financial advice, this is the figure that I submitted to the Civil Rights staff as final agreement for the compensatory damages of this settlement.

I faxed this settlement amount to Harry around 3:00PM that day. It took only one day for the Civil Rights staff to agree with this figure. I couldn't believe it was so easy this time. Harry called me and said. "I will prepare the settlement agreement and fax you a copy for your signature". I thought to myself, "what I don't have to go to some office or meeting to settle this"? I am going to settle this case right here from my fax machine?

Well come to found out, that's just what happened.

On November 11, 1998 Harry faxed me this one page settlement agreement which was very cut and dry. I read it carefully and it was self-explanatory, so I signed it and faxed it back the same day. Funny, it looked just like the other settlement agreement that I had signed six months earlier.

Harry called me as soon as he received my fax and told me, how sorry he was that I had been put through so much severe mental cruelty and to make me feel better he said, 'Mr. Johnson in my 12 years with the civil Rights Division, this is undoubtedly the largest settlement agreement I have ever seen awarded to a single individual". He also said, "Mr. Johnson you deserve every penny of it too"!

On December 12, 1998, just in time for Christmas, I received via Federal Express, the six-figure check from the U.S. Treasury.

I felt then as I do to this very day, that this compensation was duly owed to me for the illegal treatment and discrimination that I suffered at the hands of my employer.

IN CONCLUSION

To this day I still see my psychiatrist twice a month for Psychotherapy, which I will continue to do for the rest of my life. I still suffer from Agoraphobia and often have severe anxiety attacks for which I will have to take medication for the rest of my life to control. I will also have to take three types of anti-depressants a day to control my extreme depressive disorder.
I sometimes have to take sleeping medication to help with the extreme nightmares that I will have to suffer with for the rest of my life.

All these conditions and disorders are still the direct result from the illegal treatment and discrimination I received from the United States Federal Government.

What you have just read is the actual facts of what happened to me while employed at the USDA, and what I had to do in order to protect my Civil Rights as a United States Citizen. The worst and most horrendous part of this biography is none of the administrative officers or subordinates were ever punished for what they did to me. They are all still employed by the United States Government, receiving promotions and pay increases. I am a total wreck and living on disability.

www.ingramcontent.com/pod-product-compliance
Lightning Source LLC
LaVergne TN
LVHW040201080526
838202LV00042B/3269